AF615369

RING OF MEN

BY ADAM OLIENSIS

★

★

DRAMATISTS
PLAY SERVICE
INC.

©Copyright, 1995, by Adam Oliensis

CAUTION: Professionals and amateurs are hereby warned that RING OF MEN is subject to a royalty. It is fully protected under the copyright laws of the United States of America, and of all countries covered by the International Copyright Union (including the Dominion of Canada and the rest of the British Commonwealth), and of all countries covered by the Pan-American Copyright Convention and the Universal Copyright Convention, and of all countries with which the United States has reciprocal copyright relations. All rights, including professional, amateur, motion picture, recitation, lecturing, public reading, radio broadcasting, television, video or sound taping, all other forms of mechanical or electronic reproduction, such as information storage and retrieval systems and photocopying, and the rights of translation into foreign languages, are strictly reserved. Particular emphasis is laid upon the question of readings, permission for which must be secured from the author's agent in writing.

The stage performance rights in RING OF MEN (other than first class rights) are controlled exclusively by the DRAMATISTS PLAY SERVICE, INC., 440 Park Avenue South, New York, N.Y. 10016. No professional or non-professional performance of the play (excluding first class professional performance) may be given without obtaining in advance the written permission of the DRAMATISTS PLAY SERVICE, INC., and paying the requisite fee.

All inquires concerning rights should be addressed to Crying Outloud Productions, Attn: Adam Oliensis, 392 Central Park West, #7A, New York, N.Y. 10025.

SPECIAL NOTE

Anyone receiving permission to produce RING OF MEN is required (1) to give credit to the author as sole and exclusive author of the play in all programs distributed in connection with performances of the play and in all instances in which the title of the play appears for purposes of advertising, publicizing or otherwise exploiting the play and/or a production thereof; the name of the author must appear on a separate line, in which no other name appears, immediately beneath the title and in size of type equal to 50% of the largest letter used for the title of the play, and (2) to give the following acknowledgment in all programs distributed in connection with performances of the Play:

Originally produced on January 11, 1991, by Willow Cabin Theatre Company Artistic Director, Edward Berkeley; Producing Directors Adam Oliensis and Maria Radman, at the William Redfield Theatre in New York City.

For my father, some of whose wildness
and a bit of whose tenderness I hope
have found their way into this play.

RING OF MEN was produced by the Group of Eight at the Acting Studio, in New York City, on September 28, 1994. It was directed by Eileen Myers and the production stage manager, was Tess Healy. The cast was as follows:

CRAIG .... Tony Tucci
JOE .... Sean Quinn
MIKE .... David Auerbach

RING OF MEN was produced as part of Ensemble Studio Theatre's 1993 Spring One-Act Marathon (Curt Dempster, Artistic Director), in New York City, on May 19, 1993. It was directed by Jamie Richards; the set design was by H. Peet Foster; the lighting design was by Greg MacPherson. and the production stage manager was Mark Roberts. The cast was as follows:

CRAIG .... Michael Wells
JOE .... Corey Parker
MIKE .... Jesse Martin

RING OF MEN was originally produced by Willow Cabin Theatre Company (Edward Berkeley, Artistic Director; Adam Oliensis and Maria Radman, Producing Directors) in an evening titled DOUBLE BOUND, at the William Redfield Theatre in New York City on January 11, 1991. The direction and set design were by Adam Oliensis; the lighting design was by Laura Manteuffel and the production stage manager was Ira Mont. The cast was as follows:

CRAIG .... Craig Zakarian
JOE .... Chuck Simmons
MIKE. .... John Billeci

CHARACTERS

CRAIG
JOE
MIKE

TIME

Saturday afternoon. Late last Spring.

PLACE

Central Park, New York.

RING OF MEN

SCENE 1

Lights up. Two guys, both in their twenties, hanging out at a park bench. It is afternoon of a Saturday, late spring. Both wear blue jeans and identical plain white T-shirts. They wear either leather jackets or jean-jackets. Not exactly the same but similar. There is a long pause. Joe is pacing, his mind, such as it is, elsewhere. Craig is lighting up a cigarette.

CRAIG. Mike say he was coming?

JOE. I don't know, man. I don't know. Yeah, yeah. He said he was.

CRAIG. He bringing beer?

JOE. How would I know? *(Pause.)*

CRAIG. Hey ... look at that one. *(He watches.)* Skirt like that, man. I don't know. I don't know. *(Pause.)* Look at her. Legs! Jesus! Would I like to — *(He gestures.)* Jesus. *(Pause.)* Do you see that?

JOE. Yeah. Yeah, she's nice.

CRAIG. Nice? Nice doesn't begin, man. Nice doesn't begin! *(Pause.)* Siddown, man. Stop all that walking around! Relax a little, enjoy the sun! *(Joe sits. Beat. He imitates Craig's position, bathing in the sun. Pause.)* Cigarette?

JOE. *(Getting up.)* Hey, man. I gotta ask you something.

CRAIG. Siddown

JOE. This is gonna sound kinda weird.

CRAIG. Really.

JOE. You won't make funna me or nothin'? If I ask you this? I gotta ask you.
CRAIG. What.
JOE. You won't make fun?
CRAIG. I don't know, man. You gotta ask me first.
JOE. But I mean, like, will you answer me like from not goofin' on me or, or bustin' me? I mean, I gotta ask you somethin', man.
CRAIG. Yeah?.
JOE. You'll be cool with me?
CRAIG. ... Cool with you.
JOE. *(Sits close to Craig on bench. Very confidential.)* Have ... have I gotten smaller since she left me?... I mean, have I ... gotten smaller?
CRAIG. ... Whaddya mean?
JOE. I don't know. It's just this feeling. Like, like she took somethin', ya know? Like I got smaller.
CRAIG. You mean your dick?
JOE. No! No.
CRAIG. What are you saying?
JOE. What I said.
CRAIG. Smaller?
JOE. Yeah. I mean, like I feel a lot smaller, ya know?
CRAIG. ... I don't know.
JOE. You think she might come back?
CRAIG. Enjoy the sun.
JOE. *(He sits like Craig. Pause.)* I feel.... It's ... I don't know.
CRAIG. OK. Picture this. You know those big green dinosaurs? You know the ones?
JOE. Which ones?
CRAIG. You know the ones they have up at the museum, you know, the big one in the lobby?
JOE. Yeah.
CRAIG. Well, how do they know they were green?
JOE. What?
CRAIG. How do they know they were green?
JOE. I don't know.
CRAIG. That's my point.

JOE. Oh.

CRAIG. I mean, what. Did they find their skin? I don't think so. And if they did, I don't think it was still green. So how do they know they were green? *(Pause. Joe works on this.)* And another thing.

JOE. Yeah?

CRAIG. OK. They were huge, right?

JOE. Yeah.

CRAIG. Like really really huge. And they had brains the size of like a walnut, right?

JOE. How do they know that?

CRAIG. Everyone knows that.

JOE. I didn't know that.

CRAIG. Well, everyone else knows it.

JOE. Yeah?

CRAIG. They found their, you know, like their heads — skulls, and they could tell by the size of the holes in their heads, you know, inside the skulls, how big their brains were. And they were small, like the size of a walnut.

JOE. Yeah?

CRAIG. Yeah. *(Pause.)*

JOE. So what's your point?

CRAIG. 'The fuck do I know!! *(Pause. Joe is cowed.)* Just that how do they know they were green?... And they had these tiny brains. *(Pause.)*

JOE. Hunh.

CRAIG. And now they're extinct. *(Pause.)*

JOE. How'd they get that way?

CRAIG. The Earth got too hot! *(Pause.)*

JOE. I got a sore throat. *(Pause.)*

Blackout

SCENE 2

Craig and Joe are stripped down to their identical T-shirts. Craig is surreptitiously eyeing Joe's shirt.

JOE. *(Already way into the thick of this speech which has been going on for some time.)* She took my heart, man. I'm telling you she took it. She took it and stomped it and danced on it and then she just didn't like the sound that came out, like the way you just don't like a song that comes on the jukebox, and she just walked off the dance floor, man. She just walked off the floor 'cause she didn't like the song.... And she didn't say nothin'. She sure as shit didn't invite me to go to the bar with her, to get a drink or nothin'. She just walked, man, whoosh gone, danced on my heart and walked, man she just walked! *(Pause.)* I wish she'd come back. *(Long pause.)* I got a sore throat, man. I don't feel too good. *(Rubs his chest. Pause.)* Mike coming?

CRAIG. I think so.

JOE. I'm telling you, man, I feel ... I feel a lot ... smaller. *(Pause.)*

CRAIG. Lemme ask you something, man.

JOE. What?

CRAIG. Where'd you get that T-shirt?

JOE. Whaddya mean?

CRAIG. Where'd you get it?

JOE. I don't know.

CRAIG. I think it's mine.

JOE. Fuck you, man. My throat hurts.

CRAIG. I lost a T-shirt, I think playing basketball a while ago. Looked like that one.

JOE. It's a T-shirt, man.

CRAIG. I know. And I lost one just like it.

JOE. It's the same as the one you're wearing.

CRAIG. But it's the same as the one I lost.

JOE. So?

CRAIG. So, I think maybe it's mine.

JOE. This one's mine.
CRAIG. You sure?... It looks like mine.
JOE. It looks like the one you got on.
CRAIG. So?
JOE. So maybe it's the one you got on and not the one you lost!
CRAIG. What!
JOE. If this one looks like the one you lost and so you think it's that one, and this one looks like the one you got on, then maybe the one you lost is the one you got on. *(Mike enters with brown paper bag which holds six-pack. He is dressed a bit more formally than the other two, though still casually, perhaps in shirt and tie and jeans.)*
MIKE. Hey, you guys.
JOE. Hey, Mike!
CRAIG. Mike! How's it goin'?
MIKE. Sorry I'm late. I couldn't get outta the store.
JOE. No problem.
CRAIG. Don't sweat it.
MIKE. You can't believe the shit that's comin' down.
CRAIG. Always, man.
JOE. Always.
MIKE. No. I mean today on the way here, man. I mean I am completely unnerved by this fucking city.
JOE. It's a fuckin' jungle, man.
CRAIG. No shit.
MIKE. A jungle doesn't begin to describe it. Like, old monkeys. What do they do? They don't fuckin' kill each other do they?
JOE. I don't know.
MIKE. I mean what do they do? They sit in a tree, right? Which is what you think of an old monkey doing. I mean, if you're thinking of old monkeys, right?
CRAIG. Sure.
MIKE. So, I'm driving down here, and on 69th Street there's this old lady crossing the street, real slow, and against the light, and as she crosses past my car, she's past me now —

JOE. Yeah?

MIKE. I start to pull into the intersection. She looks up at me, real startled like, and like I'm gonna hit her only I won't. So I lean out the window and say, "It's OK lady. I won't hit you." Then she says, I mean she's this old lady, with a cane. She says, "Fuck you!"

JOE. She says that?

MIKE. Yeah, right? So, without thinking, I yell, "Fuck you too, lady!" I mean, I'm in a hurry to get here. It's gonna be summer. It's Saturday. I wanna catch the last of the afternoon sun. The babes still come here. This is where I'm in a hurry to get, right? I yell, "Fuck you too, lady! Fuck you twice!"

CRAIG. Whoah.

MIKE. I know, right?

CRAIG. You shouldn't ought to yell that at an old lady.

MIKE. I know! But she's just yelled at me and she's against the light and I'm pulling out real polite and all. And it just comes flying out, like without permission or anything. *(Pause. Mike paces, trying to walk off the event. It's as though he's finished with the story. Then:)* Then. As I'm yelling this, this other car — this big white Buick crunches the old lady. I mean, hits her good. Knocks her off her pins. I yell, "Fuck you twice!" she goes down like a stone. I look. And you know wha —

JOE. — Was she all right?

MIKE. Who?

JOE. The old lady.

MIKE. Yeah, yeah. I don't know. A busted leg is all. But the thing is you know who hit her?

JOE. *(Overlapping with above.)* A busted leg?

MIKE. You know who hit her?

CRAIG. Who?

MIKE. This other old lady! Could have been her fucking sister — her fucking what, her canasta partner — knocked her the fuck down in the middle of traffic. I mean I don't know what I'm doing yelling, "Fuck you twice" at a crippled-ol' old lady and then she gets knocked off her pins. Like, as if there's some, what, cause and you know —

CRAIG. Effect.

MIKE. Yeah, between me yelling and then down she goes! Only I didn't do it, but it's like I did it. She gets smacked by her fucking old lady sister! Some other senile blind bitch probably lives next door to her! It should be some crazed Iranian or a Panamanian, or a cabby, a drunk. I don't know. BUT THERE IT IS!... Even these old bitches are out there just nailing each other to the pavement, knocking each other down. One, two, three. Bang bang down you go! Don't get up or I'll knock you down again! *(Pause.)* I'm telling you, man. This city gets to you. It gets to you. *(Pause.)*

CRAIG. No shit, man. No shit. *(Pause. Mike is pacing. Craig is on bench.)*

JOE. *(Still rubbing his throat.)* Hey, Mike.

MIKE. Yeah.

JOE. ... I gotta ask you something.

MIKE. Yeah?

JOE. This is gonna sound kinda weird.

MIKE. Really.

JOE. Since JulieAnne left —

CRAIG. Oh, Christ.

JOE. What?

CRAIG. Here we go again! Lemme have a beer!

JOE. Shut up, man!

CRAIG. You shut up! All morning, "Since she left, man. You know. Since JulieAnne split and went to California.... Have I ... you know, have I gotten smaller? It's just a feeling man. But I gotta know. Have I gotten smaller since she left?" *(Joe starts for Craig. Craig squares off. Mike intervenes.)*

MIKE. Hold it! Easy! Easy! *(He has peeled Joe off his course and away a bit.)*

CRAIG. I'll thump him, man! All day long with this shit. "Have I gotten smaller, man?"

JOE. 'Least I know whose shirt I'm wearing!

CRAIG. Fuck you!

JOE. 'Least I'm not all bent about dinosaurs and the size of their tiny brains!

CRAIG. 'Bout the size of your midget dick! *(They start for each other again. Mike intervenes again.)*

MIKE. What are you guys? Animals? Just calm the fuck down! No more of this shit! Un'erstand? No more! OK? OK?

JOE. OK. *(Mike looks at Craig. Craig raises his hands in grudging acceptance. Pause.)* I just was asking a question.

CRAIG. Forget about it.

JOE. I mean I been down, you know? I keep wishin' she'd come back. I can't get off the floor. I just feel, like ... I don't know —

CRAIG. Smaller?

JOE. Yeah!! A lot — smaller since she left!

CRAIG. *(To Mike.)* You see?

JOE. I mean she just took my heart, man! She stomped on it! She danced on it and then walked off the floor, man. She walked —

CRAIG. Whoosh gone.

JOE. Like she just didn't like the song that came on the jukebox.

CRAIG. She just took her high heels —

JOE. And stomped all over my heart.

CRAIG. *(To Mike.)* Help me out, man. I'm gonna kill him.

JOE. I don't think she ever cared, man. I don't know. I feel ... I don't know. I got a sore throat. I feel, I don't know, a lot smaller.

MIKE. Joe.

JOE. What?

MIKE. Think about something else.

JOE. Hunh?

MIKE. You're gonna drive the whole world fucking nuts with this shit. For weeks. She's gone. There's other bitches. Relax. Enjoy the sun.

CRAIG. That's what I been telling him.

MIKE. It's good advice, man. Have a beer. Ease up. It's a beautiful day. We are here to enjoy the sun, the beer, and the company of good friends. *(Mike takes out beers. Hands them to Craig and Joe. Takes one for himself. Craig drinks right away.)*

CRAIG. Bag. *(Sip.)* Bag. *(Mike pulls out can-size brown bags. Hands them around. All three ritually pop open the bags, slide their cans inside bags, and scrunch the bags just right. Craig and Mike drink. Joe isn't ready yet. Craig belches. Mike hiccoughs and belches. Pause.)*

MIKE. Saturdays are good. *(Pause.)*

CRAIG. Yup. *(Pause.)*

MIKE. *(To Joe.)* Think about something else.

JOE. I'm trying.

CRAIG. Just a six?

MIKE. It'll get warm otherwise. We'll go for more. *(To Joe.)* Drink your beer.

JOE. *(Opening his, but not drinking.)* I'm not thirsty.

MIKE. Drink your beer.

JOE. I got a sore throat.

CRAIG. From eating too much pussy.

JOE. Fuck you.

MIKE. *(Puts on sunglasses.)* Ever notice how blondes come out when it's sunny?

CRAIG. Where?

MIKE. *(Points.)* Over there. When it's cloudy, what do they all gotta stay inside? Is it a rule? Where do they go?

CRAIG. Her hair is dyed.

JOE. Where?

MIKE. There. Through the trees.

CRAIG. She's a fake.

JOE. I don't see her.

MIKE. Right there. To the left of the thing.

JOE. What thing?

MIKE. The jungle gym.

JOE. *(Looks hard.)* The blonde?

MIKE. Yeah.

JOE. With the hair?

CRAIG. It's dyed.

JOE. She's beautiful.

CRAIG. She's a fake.

JOE. *(Overlapping.)* So what? Wow.

MIKE. *(Overlapping.)* No, she isn't.

CRAIG. What.

MIKE. Fake.

CRAIG. It's dyed.

MIKE. That don't make it fake. *(Pause.)* Is it saying it isn't?
CRAIG. It isn't what.
MIKE. Dyed —
JOE. Look at the way the sun is on it.
MIKE. — Her hair.
JOE. It's like, like ...
MIKE. Spun gold.
JOE. Spun gold!
MIKE. Is it, you know, making any claims?
JOE. LOOK at that WALK!
CRAIG. What are you fucking talking about?
MIKE. I'm saying it's not making any claims.
CRAIG. Her hair?
MIKE. So it's not fake. It's just blonde.
CRAIG. But it's dyed!
MIKE. But it's not *saying* it's not. So it's not *fake* it's just *dyed.*
JOE. Spun gold! ... I don't think I ever seen spun gold.
MIKE. Well, that's what it looks like. *(Pause.)*
JOE. Whaddya think her name is?
CRAIG. Shut up!
JOE. Fuck you!
MIKE. She's somethin'.
JOE. I think her name is ...
MIKE. Vicki.
JOE. ... Cassandra.
CRAIG. Her name is WHORE!
JOE. Fuck you!
MIKE. What makes you so sure?
CRAIG. They all are.
JOE. Not her.
MIKE. For that ...
JOE. I'd walk backwards on my ass —
MIKE. Across a desert.
JOE. Full of broken glass.
CRAIG. She's a fuckin' fake.
MIKE. You know, Craig, you are filling the atmosphere full of some extremely negative vibrations on this fine day.
CRAIG. *(To Joe.)* Forget about JulieAnne already? You

fucking dildo! "Have I gotten smaller? Hunh, Craig? Since she left, have I gotten smaller?"

MIKE. Leave him alone, man.

CRAIG. I'm just saying, it can't be all that bad if a fake whore can ease it up so quick.

JOE. Hey!

CRAIG. What? *(Joe indicates in direction he was looking. He sits, pulls out shades. Now all three sit on bench with sunglasses on. They are like birds on a wire. Craig pointedly ignores her. Joe and Mike watch. Craig is L., Mike is C., Joe is R. Though she never appears, we watch the three guys watch her approach from L, and pass in front of them D. Mike and Joe nod and mutter awkward acknowledgments, "Hey." "Hello." "Hey, baby." She goes on by. Silence as the two watch her going off into distance R. Finally:)*

MIKE. She wanted me.

JOE. She was looking at ME.

MIKE. No no no no no no no. She felt SAFE pretending she might have been looking at you. She was LOOKING at ME.

JOE. Bullshit, man. *(Craig is up behind bench. Now looking after her.)*

MIKE. I'm tellin' you, man. The chemistry scared her, like a doe blinded by the headlights of my radiant charisma. She is at my mercy now. She is doomed. Beyond hope! All that's left to fulfill now is the sweet taste of her actual surrender.

JOE. Which you may or may not —

MIKE. Induce. According to my whim.

CRAIG. Fuck.

JOE. *(Regarding Mike.)* I suppose I am forced to accede before a superior power?

MIKE. I think so.

CRAIG. You're both fucking ignorant!

MIKE. What, she wanted you?

CRAIG. Why are you always so fucking stupid? Don't you have a fucking clue? 'Sittin' here with you two bozos! Fuck, what am I doing?

JOE. Hey, Craig.

CRAIG. What?

JOE. You got a better place to go? *(Pause.)* Hey, Craig.... You got some better place to go?

CRAIG. *(Going for Joe with Mike intervening again.)* Up your fucking face I'm going, you dipshit-weasil-motherfucker!

MIKE. *(Overlapping.)* Hey, hey, hey, hey! *(Craig chases around bench after Joe. Joe runs, keeping Mike between Craig and himself.)*

JOE. A lot of fucking fashion models just waiting to suck the paint off your house. You're just fighting them off with a couple a sticks! "No, baby, I gotta get to the park! Got a lot of 'sponsibilities hanging with Mike and Joe! Sorry, baby. I'll fuck you good later, but right now I got my obligations, baby!"

MIKE. *(To Joe.)* Shut up!

JOE. Lot of 'sponsibilities, baby!

MIKE. What's the fucking matter with you! *(Smacks Joe on head.)*

JOE. I'm sick of this shit! I can't say anything without, "Shut up, Joe! Siddown, Joe! Think about something else, Joe!"

CRAIG. Oh, shut up!

JOE. See? See! All day long! Anything I got to say! Anything I gotta ask! "Shut up, Joe!" I'M FUCKING SICK OF IT!

CRAIG. The bitch left! She went to California! She's gone! There's other bitches! GET OVER IT!! *(Long pause.)*

JOE. Where'd she go?

CRAIG. What?

JOE. Where'd you say JulieAnne went?

CRAIG. ... I don't know.

JOE. You said she went to California.

CRAIG. Did she?

JOE. Did you?

CRAIG. I don't know.

JOE. That's what you said. *(To Mike.)* That's what he said. You heard him. He said she went there!

MIKE. *(To Craig.)* That's where she went?

CRAIG. How the fuck would I know where she went?

JOE. That's what I'm asking! Why'd you say she went to California?

CRAIG. 'Ts where I'd go! Anywhere to get the fuck away from you!
JOE. She didn't tell you?
CRAIG. Why would she tell me?
JOE. She might have said something.
CRAIG. She didn't say anything!
JOE. She might have known some guy out there I didn't know about. She might have told you.
CRAIG. Hey, man, why would she tell me anything!
JOE. You might have talked to her!
CRAIG. I didn't talk to her.
JOE. OK. I'm just asking. *(Pause.)*
MIKE. Drink your beer.
JOE. I just thought you might have talked to her. *(Pause.)* I thought maybe you know where she was. Maybe you know and you weren't telling me. Maybe, you know, you know some things that you're not telling me. I don't know. I'm asking, that's all.
CRAIG. Forget about it.
JOE. I'm asking 'cause I'd wanna know. I mean, I miss her, you know? And if I could know where she was, you know?... *(Pause. Joe is choked up with tears.)* I'd wanna ... wanna talk to her.
MIKE. You don't wanna talk to her.
JOE. I do, man. I wanna talk to her.
MIKE. She's gone, man.
JOE. I know she's gone. And I wanna talk to her. I miss her.
MIKE. You don't miss her.
JOE. I'd walk through fire for her! Across that — that river!
MIKE. What river?
JOE. With all the bones and the ghosts! And then drag her back! Past the guy on the ferry and the monsters 'n everything!
MIKE. What!
JOE. Like whatsisname!
MIKE. Who??
JOE. *(Struggling.)* Wh ... wh.... Whatisname!

MIKE. Who's that?
JOE. If I knew that, would I be calling him whatsisname?!
CRAIG. It's not JulieAnne, you know.
JOE. Right. It's Myrna Loy.
CRAIG. Another bitch will fill the gap.
MIKE. Or be the gap to fill.
CRAIG. Some other one comes along, JulieAnne will be like — like ...
MIKE. — the Mariah winds, an eerie whistling in your ear, faintly reminiscent of a turbulent but only dimly remembered storm in the night.
JOE. 'T fuck?
CRAIG. You saw the way you were looking at that blonde walked by. Did you see that, Mike?
MIKE. The blonde wanted ME.
CRAIG. That goes without saying. But you saw —
JOE. I didn't agree to that.
MIKE. It was obvious.
CRAIG. You're both fucking ignorant.
MIKE. We're finishing up the blonde!
CRAIG. Which is my point!
JOE. What!
CRAIG. The blonde! Joe. Did you see the way you were looking at the blonde?
MIKE. I saw.
CRAIG. So, you start touching her. You start kissing her. You sleep a couple o' nights with your head nestled between her tits, you know what I'm saying? Before you know it —
JOE. I was just looking at her!
CRAIG. Now!
MIKE. She wanted me.
CRAIG. Or someone else. It could be someone else! Anyone else is what I'm saying. JulieAnne split! You find another one makes you feel good, JulieAnne is so far back in the archives you gotta use a history book to find her fucking birthday!... You're on top of this new one —
JOE. The blonde?
CRAIG. Any new one! Anyone! And you're thinking

JulieWho? You could fall into her eyes, but I can't remember. Her ass in my hands — the way she moved when she came. What did that feel like?

JOE. You're sick!

CRAIG. I used to kiss her under her ribs and she'd go wild! Who cares! — and meantime the new bitch —

JOE. Where'd you kiss her?

CRAIG. Meantime the new bitch —

JOE. — Where'd you kiss her?

CRAIG. What?

JOE. JulieAnne.

CRAIG. What. Under here. *(He points to a spot halfway between his solar plexus and short ribs.)* Anywhere. You bite her, kiss her there, you know work your way down ...

JOE. How do you know?

CRAIG. With the new bitch —

JOE. *(To Mike.)* — You heard him.

CRAIG. — They all like that —

JOE. She told you I would do that?

CRAIG. One's like another!

JOE. I'm not this fucking dumb! You! You fucking traitor —

CRAIG. I'm just saying!

JOE. *(To Mike.)* You heard what he's saying!

CRAIG. You are the lamest fucking fuck.

JOE. She told you how I'd do that?

CRAIG. What!!

JOE. What did she do? Did she tell you? Tell me she told you. Tell me, man. You'd better tell me she told you.

CRAIG. *(Overlap.)* She didn't have to.

MIKE. *(Overlap.)* Hey hey hey hey hey hey. *(Mike has gotten their attention and motions R. where blonde, again off-stage, is coming into their view. They stop the action of their fight to act casual and very very cool as she walks by. This time Mike is definitely the star while Craig and Joe are fuming, not really looking at her. As she passes D.:)* Sweetheart — *(Joe has sidled over near to Craig and viciously sucker punches him in the jaw, a shot that echoes a resounding "crack." Craig goes down like a stone, unconscious.)*

JOE. *(His hand in pain and heart in fury.)* Aaahhhhhhooooooouuuwwww!

MIKE. WHAT!

JOE. *(At Craig's inert body.)* YOU WERE FUCKING HER, YOU FUCKING FUCK! HE WAS FUCKING JULIEANNE!!

MIKE. What are you talking about!

JOE. You heard him! You heard him! He knew what to do to her! She didn't tell him! He knew how to do it!

MIKE. You knocked him out!

JOE. I'll do it again! I'll do it again! I'll knockout the whole fucking world!

MIKE. Shut up!

JOE. *(At the sky, the trees, the passers by, the world at large.)* I'LL KNOCK YOU OUT! YOU HEAR ME! I'LL FUCKING PUNCH YOUR LIGHTS OUT, RATTLE YOUR WINDOWS! I'LL SHATTER YOU!!

MIKE. SHUT UP! JOE SHUT UP! *(Mike slaps Joe in the face. Joe is silenced. Pause. By way of apologetic explanation.)* You ruined the thing with the blonde. I was gonna close in for the thing, you gotta sucker punch him. This is gettin' to be a fucked up Saturday, man, a very fucked up Saturday. *(Mike is going to Craig and props him up to semi-half-sitting while he wipes blood off Craig's lip with a handkerchief. Craig is slowly beginning to come to.)*

JOE. He was fucking JulieAnne.

MIKE. How you know this?

JOE. He knew what she liked — about kissing her ribs.

MIKE. So?

JOE. An' how you could fall in at her eyes.

MIKE. *(Laughing.)* And you think this is, what, some kind of unique evidence that he was fucking her?

JOE. She was givin' those eyes away!

MIKE. You think every chick in the world doesn't like the same shit?! You think whatsername — what are you, fucking cherry?!

JOE. I can tell, man! I can tell!

MIKE. You can tell! He's your friend. You don't swing until you know!

JOE. My hand hurts.

CRAIG. *(Only about 8 percent conscious.)* I'll be down in a minute, mom.
MIKE. Oh, you got him good.
JOE. He knows where she is and what she's like when she comes, and — and about fallin' in at her eyes!
MIKE. It's one chick or another! Ain't you ever been laid otherwise? You think the thing with you and JulieAnne was any different than, what, any farmer and his dried up wife?
CRAIG. Oh, man, somebody turn down the radio.
MIKE. You all right?
CRAIG. The fuck happened?
MIKE. That blonde is a knockout, hunh?
CRAIG. What?
JOE. I punched you in your head.
CRAIG. ... Why?
JOE. You were fucking JulieAnne.
MIKE. *He* thinks you were fucking JulieAnne.
JOE. Where is she now? *(Pause.)*
CRAIG. California.
MIKE. How do you know this?
CRAIG. Fuck you, Mike.
JOE. Where in California?
CRAIG. San Francisco.
JOE. You got an address?
CRAIG. No.
JOE. Phone number?
CRAIG. In my jacket. *(Joe goes to Craig's jacket on bench and rifles the pockets. Mike and Craig are together on the ground. Joe finds scrap of paper.)*
JOE. She staying with someone?
CRAIG. Some guy she knows. An actor.
JOE. Fuck.
MIKE. You gonna call her?
JOE. I don't know.
CRAIG. Don't call her.
JOE. I gotta talk to her.
CRAIG. No, you don't.
JOE. Why were you doin' that?

CRAIG. ... I don't know.

JOE. I gotta talk to her. *(Joe goes to exit. Stops.)* Craig.

CRAIG. What?

JOE. ... Why were you doin' that? *(Craig doesn't answer.)* Since we're fifteen. You guys ... I mean, without you guys....Why'd you have to go an' do that? *(Pause. Joe goes to exit again.)*

CRAIG. Why'd I do that, Mike?

MIKE. That's what he's askin' you.

CRAIG. Whyn't *you* tell 'im, Mike? Why'd I do that, Mike? Why'd I do that? Tell him, Mike! WHY'D I DO THAT?

MIKE. 'The fuck would I know? *(Pause. Joe realizes. Sits on the ground. Pause.)* What? You think.... Don't look at me.

CRAIG. She told me.

MIKE. What. Before or after you banged her in the ass?

CRAIG. Fuck you.

MIKE. She's a cunt. *(Joe gets up to leave. At this point the light begins to fade at an imperceptible rate until, by the end of the play it is dusk in the park — dusk with a touch of moonlight or streetlight.)* What. Joe, have a beer, man. You gonna let some three-thousand-mile-away bitch fuck up our Saturday afternoon?

JOE. *(To both.)* You make me sick.

MIKE. *(Overlap.)* I introduced you to her!

CRAIG. *(Overlap.)* 'Cause you found out what she was like?

JOE. What you're like.

CRAIG. 'Cause you found out what you made believe you didn't know?

JOE. Hey! If I woulda known —

CRAIG. She woulda left anyway!

JOE. — if I'd a known about you!!

CRAIG. If you'd a known about me what! That I like to fuck? That if a chick's begging and she gives me a hard on, I'll fuck her?! You known that about me since we're fifteen!

JOE. *(Overlapping Craig's last sentence.)* Don't say that about JulieAnne!

CRAIG. That she gave me a hard on?

JOE. Shut up!!

CRAIG. That she begged? 'Cause that's what she did!

JOE. Fuck you!!

CRAIG. "Please, Craig, please! Give it to me now, Craig! Deeper, Craig! PLEASE!" You think your midget dick is the only one ever — *(Joe goes for Craig. They scuffle. There's a headlock, a couple short rabbit punches, finally a takedown with Craig on top. It's all happened very fast, too fast for Mike to intervene. This is brutal, unceremonious street violence, not a drawn out stage fight. Craig is holding Joe down on his back, kneeling over him. There is some blood on their faces.)* You think I don't wanna think it's just me? You think you're the only one disappointed? You think I don't wish JulieAnne wanted only me?... Grow up! They like men, that's the point, isn't it? Not just you, not just me! Anyone! Be a man! Get over it! They want you to own 'em, an' then they run away! Where? Where do you think? Don't be fuckin' stupid! And don't blame me for the way it is; it's what they do! Don't you fuckin' blame me for it! *(Craig gets off him. Joe lies there on his back. Pause. Joe crinkles and lobs the phone number a ways away from himself. Craig is standing at a distance. Mike sits on bench. Joe remains supine. Long pause. Mike gives Joe handkerchief.)*

MIKE. Joe.... Hey , look.... That's what she was like. Before she even left whatsisname, the Spanish guy — When I introduced you to her. Remember? Club Mars? I was doin' her, he was doin' her. Wipe your face. She was fun. Who knew you were gonna go all stupid for her? So, that's a reason I should stop? I was havin' fun, you were havin' fun —

JOE. Everyone was havin' fun.

MIKE. So, you went stupid for her. It could happen to anyone. I warned you from the beginning. She's fun, just don't go stupid —

JOE. I loved her.

MIKE. ... You tell me the difference. *(Pause.)*

JOE. *(Still on his back.)* See, but what I don't understand ... how can she — how could she give that ... to more than one person?

CRAIG. It's sex, man.

JOE. Just, like, just dicks and pussies and, I gotta come inside somethin' warm tonight or I won't sleep good.

CRAIG. Pretty much.

JOE. And me thinking it was somethin' more —

CRAIG. You can think whatever you want.

JOE. But I'd be wrong.

CRAIG. 'Pparently.

JOE. And it's just you or me or you —

MIKE. Or some guy in California.

JOE. And under, you know, the big sky, it doesn't make any difference to her.

CRAIG. Or to you.

MIKE. Or it makes all the difference in the world, until later when it doesn't. And then later it does again ... that it's somebody else.

JOE. See, but ... I don't know.

CRAIG. What?

JOE. I don't know.... It's just, you know, when she'd be ... sleeping? I'd wake up and she'd have her hand ... *(He puts his hand on his chest.)* And there she'd be, dreaming, just this ... almost like there was moonlight coming off her skin. Like ... not shining —

MIKE. Luminous.

JOE. ... Luminous. And I'd lay real still with those beautiful ... luminous ... long arms and legs. Around me. And her hands ...

MIKE. Yeah?

JOE. A little smaller than you'd think they'd be, you know?

CRAIG. I don't know.

JOE. And when she was dreaming or falling asleep they were sort of ... busy, these little twitches, one finger at a time, like they were trying to say something to someone or hold on to something that wasn't really too nearby and she didn't even know the shape or feel of. And, you know, when they were working like that, her hands, I always thought ... I always kinda believed that even though she was dreamin', that she was tryin' to send a message through to me in some kinda special code that I didn't understand but that's what woke me up, this code she was sending from inside of her dream to mine. And my dream understood it and it yelled out to me, "Hey, BOZO, don't sleep through this!" She loves you. So wake up and look outta the window, because underneath the moon and all those stars, almost all of which you can't even see, and under all those skyscrapers across the river, and brownstones, and street lights and windows, lighted ones and black ones, and in a city this big with alla these people, sleepin' and awake, in a country this size in a world so ... round, this beautiful lady, this, this luminous long lady ... wrapped all around you in her quiet sleep is sending you a secret code with her little hands that she loves you and that she belongs to you and that you have a, a, special place under all the stars and buildings and windows and people, one special place in her dreams where you belong and no-one else does. And you bumped into it all accidental-like at Club Mars ... *(Here Joe may begin to raise himself slowly to sitting and include Mike and Craig more in his questions.)* An' now I don't know anything about what all that was. About the code or the moon or her dreams or mine. An' I don't know how she could give that away to everyone or anyone because it's a million miles away up there with the stars I can't even see. Or did I just make that up an' maybe I was always all the time all by myself for alla that, or did she believe it too then, or never, or what?... Is it all just that I ... was I just stupid for her? *(The three remain motionless: Joe looking up at what is by now becoming a night sky; Mike on the bench looking out; Craig, D.R. facing away and now for the first time mourning JulieAnne. Pause.)*

MIKE. She's a very charming lady.

CRAIG. It could happen to anyone. *(Pause. Slow fade to black.)*

PROPERTY LIST

Cigarette (CRAIG)
Lighter or matches (CRAIG)
Brown paper bag (MIKE) with:
  six-pack of beer
  can-size paper bags
3 pairs of sunglasses (CRAIG, MIKE, JOE)
Handkerchief (MIKE)
Cardboard and aluminum sun reflector (CRAIG)
Basketball

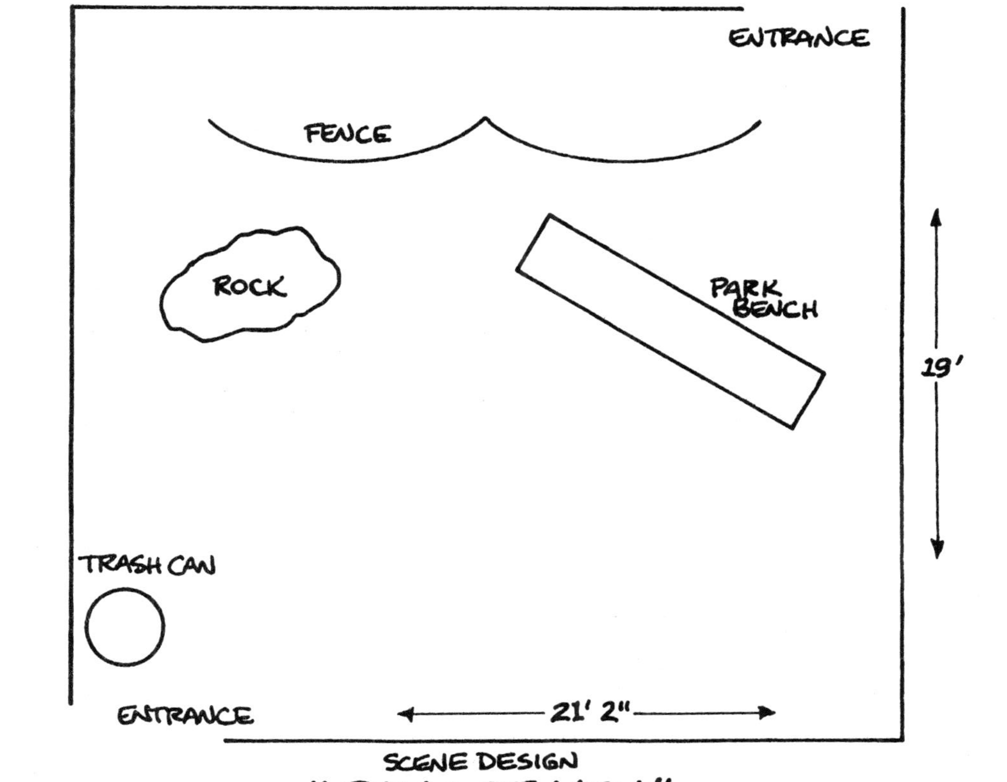

SCENE DESIGN

"RING OF MEN"

(DESIGNED BY ADAM OLIENSIS FOR WILLOW CABIN THEATRE COMPANY)

NEW
PLAYS

THE AFRICAN COMPANY PRESENTS
RICHARD III
by Carlyle Brown

EDWARD ALBEE'S
FRAGMENTS and THE MARRIAGE PLAY

IMAGINARY LIFE
by Peter Parnell

MIXED EMOTIONS
by Richard Baer

THE SWAN
by Elizabeth Egloff

Write for information as to availability

DRAMATISTS PLAY SERVICE, Inc.
440 Park Avenue South   New York, N.Y. 10016

NEW
PLAYS

THE LIGHTS
by Howard Korder

THE TRIUMPH OF LOVE
by James Magruder

LATER LIFE
by A.R. Gurney

THE LOMAN FAMILY PICNIC
by Donald Margulies

A PERFECT GANESH
by Terrence McNally

SPAIN
by Romulus Linney

Write for information as to availability

DRAMATISTS PLAY SERVICE, Inc.
440 Park Avenue South New York, N.Y. 10016

NEW PLAYS

LONELY PLANET
by Steven Dietz

THE AMERICA PLAY
by Suzan-Lori Parks

THE FOURTH WALL
by A.R. Gurney

JULIE JOHNSON
by Wendy Hammond

FOUR DOGS AND A BONE
by John Patrick Shanley

DESDEMONA, A PLAY ABOUT A HANDKERCHIEF
by Paula Vogel

Write for information as to availability

DRAMATISTS PLAY SERVICE, Inc.
440 Park Avenue South New York, N.Y. 10016